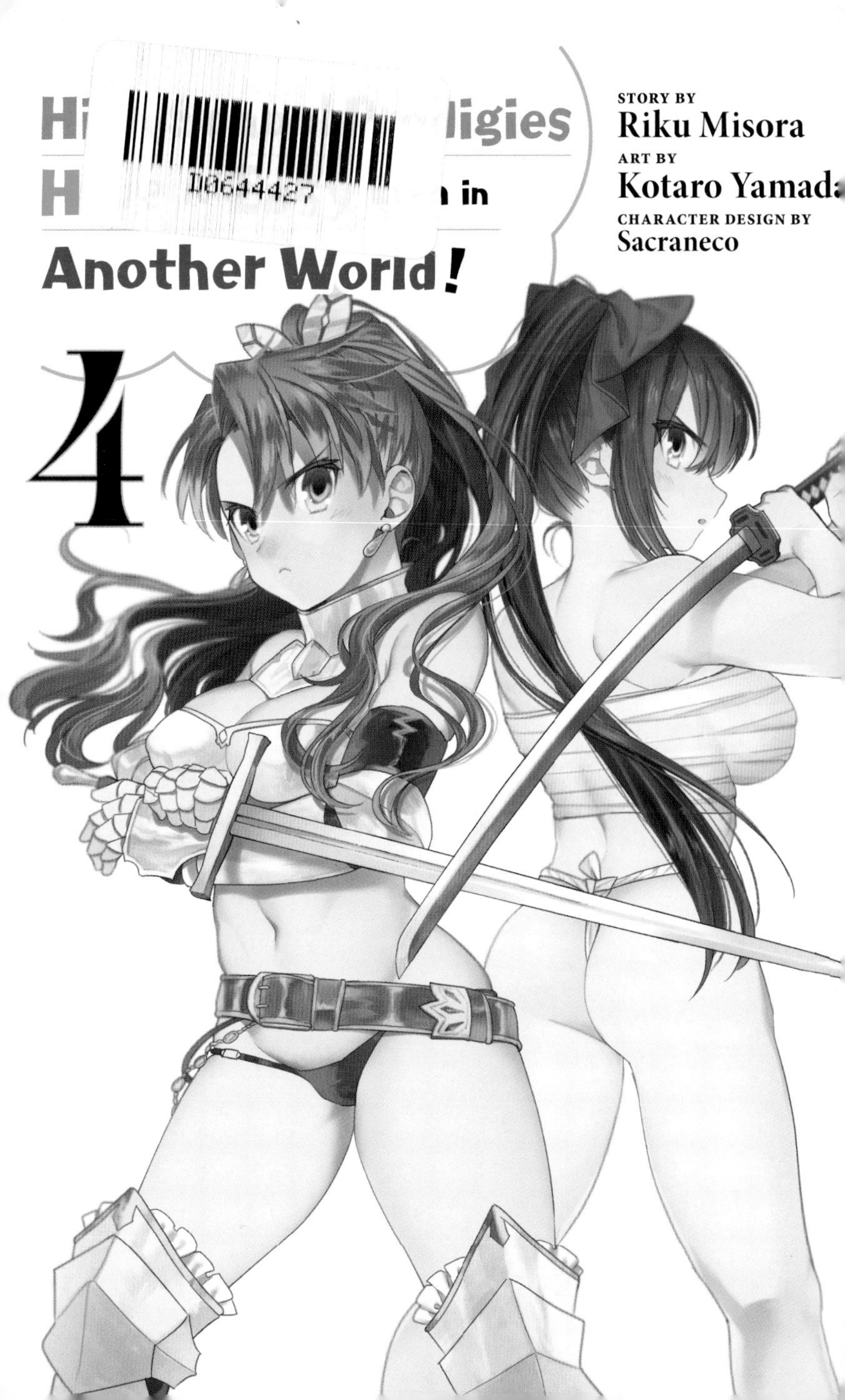
ligies
n in
Another World!
4
STORY BY
Riku Misora
ART BY
Kotaro Yamad
CHARACTER DESIGN BY
Sacraneco

CONTENTS

HIGH SCHOOL PRODIGIES HAVE IT EASY EVEN IN ANOTHER WORLD!

MAYOR'S RESIDENCE, RESIDENTIAL DISTRICT (ARISTOCRATS), DORMUNDT
WE'VE DONE RESEARCH ON THE "HEAVENLY FIRE" WARCRAFT MAGIC WIELDED BY GUSTAV, THE FASTIDIOUS DUKE.
IT ISN'T JUST A STANDARD EXPLOSIVE. IT'S MORE LIKE A FIREBOMB.

HUH. SO RATHER THAN BLOWING STUFF UP, IT BURNS EVERYTHING TO THE GROUND?
EXACTLY. IT'S NOT TOO MUCH OF A THREAT IF WE AVOID A DIRECT HIT.
AND RINGO-KUN IS ALREADY ARRANGING DEFENSIVE MEASURES.
EVEN SO, WE'VE GOT TO HAVE SOMETHING IN PLACE BEFORE WE MOBILIZE AT WINTER'S END.
I WANT EVERYONE TO READ THESE EMERGENCY MANUALS CAREFULLY. THEY'RE TO BE RELIED ON IN TIMES OF CRISIS.

CHAPTER 24: ILL-BODING FLAMES

HIGH SCHOOL
PRODIGIES HAVE
IT EASY EVEN IN
ANOTHER
WORLD!

RESIDENTIAL DISTRICT (ARISTOCRATS), DORMUNDT
TO HELL WITH THAT WHITE-HAIRED SCUM!
GAAN (CRASH)
ANGELS? YEAH, RIIIGHT!
SURE LOOK LIKE ORDINARY FREAKIN' FOLKS TO ME!
GAAN
KYLE... YOUR TEMPER'S WORSE THAN USUAL TODAY...

I DON'T BLAME HIM.
HIS FATHER WAS PROSECUTED AND THROWN IN JAIL BY THE COMMONERS.
THEY EVEN STRIPPED HIM OF HIS AUTHORITY TO RULE OVER THEIR VILLAGE, A RIGHT ORIGINALLY GRANTED TO HIM BY MARQUIS FINDOLPH.

HOWEVER... THE TIME FOR US TO COUNTER-ATTACK IS CLOSE AT HAND.

YOU SAYING YOU GOT THE GOODS?
HUH? WHAT'S THIS ABOUT?

I HAVE A DISTANT RELATIVE IN GUSTAV DOMAIN—
ONE WHO SYMPATHIZES AND WANTS TO SUPPORT OUR CAUSE...
SU (FWIP)
...WITH THESE.

WHAT IS IT? POTTERY? IF SO, IT LOOKS RATHER UNREFINED.
OF COURSE IT'S UN-REFINED.
THIS IS A BOMB THEY CALL "ROARING THUNDER," YOU SEE.
SA (LEAP)
A B-BOMB!?
KEEP IT DOWN, MORON!

GOOD JOB GETTING YOUR HANDS ON THAT. MUST'VE BEEN TOUGH SNEAKING IT IN.
A SIMPLE MATTER, AS THE COMMONERS ARE MOSTLY WARY OF NOBLES.
YOU SAYING SOME LOWLY TRASH SMUGGLED IT IN FOR YOU?
Y-YOU'VE MADE ALLIES OF SOME COMMONERS, THEN?

NOT EVERY COMMONER IS NECESSARILY ON BOARD WITH THE SEVEN LUMINARIES.
SOME ARE PARASITES WHO WOULD RATHER LEECH OFF US NOBLES...
...WHILE THERE ARE OTHERS WHO REJECT THIS NEW, COMPETITIVE SOCIETY...
IT WAS QUITE EASY, WINNING OVER THE POWERLESS.

COME SPRING, WE AND THE SUBJUGATING FORCES WILL HIT THE SEVEN LUMINARIES FROM BOTH SIDES.
CAN'T WAIT TO SEE THAT WHITE-HAIRED PUNK CRAP HIMSELF!
HA HA HA!
グビ グビ
GUBI (GULP) GUBI
HMM?
WUZZAT?

ONE OF SEVERAL SHRINES ERECTED HERE AND THERE BY THE SEVEN LUMINARIES.
SHRINE?
IT'S A WORD OF YAMATO ORIGIN.
THEY WORSHIP SOME IDOL CALLED A JIZOU BY WAY OF THESE LITTLE HUTCHES.
WHAT THE HELL?
IT DOESN'T LOOK LIKE AN IDOL.
IT'S... JUST A LITTLE CYLINDER, RIGHT?

I GOT IT FIGURED OUT! THOSE LOWLY SAVAGES DON'T HAVE THE TECHNOLOGY TO CARVE REAL STATUES...
...SO THEY JUST PLUNKED DOWN THIS BIG ROCK TO TRY AND FOOL US!
AH, A DISTINCT POSSIBILITY, YES.
GUESS WE'VE GOT NO CHOICE, HUH? THE GREAT NOBLES OF THE EMPIRE HAVE GOTTA TEACH THESE ASSHOLES A THING OR TWO ABOUT CLASS.
KYUPON (POP)
キュポン

YOU LIKE THAT? TASTY, HUH?
TOPO (GLUG)
NOT LIKE THAT STALE WORT YOU PEASANTS DRINK.
THIS HERE IS SWEET, MELLOW, FULL-BODIED BOOZE...THE CLASSIEST AROUND!
PO
TOPOPO
YOU HEARIN' ME, GODS OF THE POOR SAVAGES?
HA HA HA HA HA HA HA HA!

OFFICE OF THE WARDEN OF THE NORTH, GUSTAV DOMAIN
OH! HOW EXTRAORDINARILY BEAUTIFUL AND MAJESTIC IT IS......!
IMMORTAL-IZING HIS GRACE IN CRUDE BRONZE OR STONE? THAT WOULD BE INEXCUS-ABLE.
A STATUE OF PURE GOLD, HOWEVER, IS JUST THE THING TO MAKE THE EMPEROR'S AUTHORITY KNOWN TO THE PEOPLE...
THE STATUE WILL BE INSTALLED IN THE CENTRAL GARDENS OF THE IMPERIAL CAPITAL AT ONCE, MILORD.
HAVE THE MAIN MEANS OF TRANSPOR-TATION BEEN ARRANGED?

I WAS THINKING WE MIGHT USE THE "ELE-PHANTS"...
...THOSE BEASTS FROM THE NEW CONTINENT THAT HAVE BEEN BROUGHT OVER. A TEAM OF FOUR WILL CARRY THE STATUE.
A GROUP OF FERAL HORSES...?
VERY WELL. BUT DO ASSIGN A TROOP TO GUARD THE STATUE DURING TRANSIT. I DEMAND STRICT SURVEILLANCE.
SHOULD THERE BE EVEN A SINGLE SCRATCH ON IT, EVERY SOLDIER, ALONG WITH THEIR FAMILIES, WILL LOSE THEIR HEADS.

...UNDERSTOOD?
YES, MILORD! I WILL BE SURE TO BEAT THAT INTO THOSE IN CHARGE.
HMPH. ALSO, OSCAR...
YES, MILORD?
I HEREBY COMMISSION ANOTHER FOUR STATUES TO BE INSTALLED IN THE NORTHERN, SOUTHERN, EASTERN, AND WESTERN WARDS OF THE EMPIRE.
MAKE HASTE. WE SHALL START AMASSING THE GOLD AT ONCE.

WHAT ......!? ANOTHER FOUR? IN PURE GOLD... MILORD?

FOUR FOR NOW, YES... WHEN ALL IS SAID AND DONE, EVERY IMPERIAL DOMAIN WILL HAVE ONE ENSHRINED.
THE COMMONERS MUST UNDERSTAND THE GLORY AND MIGHT OF HIS GRACE.
N-NOT GILDED, BUT... SOLID GOLD ...!?
NATUR-ALLY.

I WILL NOT STAND FOR GILDING OR SOME OTHER FORM OF DECEPTION TO REPRESENT OUR UNDYING LOYALTY!
OR PERHAPS ...
...YOU IMAGINE MY LOYALTY ITSELF IS GILDED FOR THE SAKE OF APPEARANCES ...?

H-H-H-HEAVENS NO, MILORD!
I-I KNOW FULL WELL THAT YOUR LOYALTY TO HIS GRACE... IS UTTERLY INDISPUTABLE.
B-BUT, IF I MAY...
THIS SINGLE GOLDEN STATUE HAS ALREADY BURDENED THE PEOPLE...
SHOULD WE ASK THEM TO PRODUCE THE FUNDS FOR FOUR MORE, WELL...

—THEY'LL STARVE TO DEATH...IS THAT IT?
LET THEM.
WHAT ......!?
KNIGHTS DISPLAY THEIR FIDELITY THROUGH DEEDS IN BATTLE.
NOBLES DEMONSTRATE IT BY PROPERLY TENDING TO THEIR LANDS.
SO IN WHAT MINIMAL WAY CAN LOWBORN PEASANTS SHOW LOYALTY, IF NOT THROUGH VALOR OR WISDOM?
THERE IS BUT ONE—
THEY CAN DIE FOR HIS GRACE.

INTRINSICALLY, PRECIOUS METALS LIKE GOLD HAVE NO VALUE.
RATHER, IT REPRESENTS THE PEOPLE'S LIFEBLOOD, WRUNG FROM THEIR BODIES AND SCRAPED FROM THEIR BONES. THAT'S WHY...
...THIS GOLD STATUE HAS MEANING.
IT'S IMBUED WITH THE LOYALTY OF THE SUBJECTS WHO DWELL IN THESE LANDS.
MEANING, THE GOLD IS PROOF OF MY LOYALTY TO HIS GRACE...!
GIRO (GLARE)

...DO YOU UNDERSTAND NOW, OSCAR?
IT IS AS YOU SAY, MILORD...
...NO, THERE'S NO QUESTIONING HIS LOYALTY.
HIS DEDICATION AND DEVOTION ARE SURELY NIGH ON HEROIC.

BUT... AS A LEADER, THERE'S NO GREATER FOOL...!
GIRI (GRIT)
AT THIS PACE, ALL OF GUSTAV DOMAIN WILL BE IN RUINS WITHIN A FEW YEARS.
HIS GROTESQUE BRAND OF LOYALTY WILL END UP KILLING COMMONERS AND NOBLES ALIKE.
THAT'S WHY THE BLUE BRIGADE MUST CARRY OUT THEIR PLAN WITHOUT DELAY...!

LET'S CHANGE THE SUBJECT TO ANOTHER MATTER, OSCAR.
Y-YES!?
BIKU (JOLT)
HAS THE REBELLION IN FINDOLPH DOMAIN BEEN SUPPRESSED?
WELL, COME SPRING, OUR FORCES WILL DESCEND UPON FINDOLPH.
WE'RE ALREADY AMASSING TROOPS IN THE FOOTHILLS OF THE LE LUK MOUNTAINS.

ONCE THE ROUTES ARE CLEAR, WE'LL MARCH INTO FINDOLPH DOMAIN AND SLAUGHTER EVERY LAST REBEL.
...DID YOU JUST SAY...
..."COME SPRING"? SPRING!?
YOU'RE TELLING ME YOU'VE TAKEN NO ACTION YET!?
IT'S ALREADY BEEN AN ENTIRE MONTH SINCE I ORDERED THE SUB-JUGATING ARMY TO DEPLOY!
ZO (SHUDDER)
EEP ...!
AND YET, THOSE VERMIN STILL TRAMPLE UPON ONE OF THE HOLY DOMAINS OF OUR EMPEROR...
...AND WE ALLOW THEM TO RUN RAM-PAAANT !?!?!?
AAAH!!

WH-WHAT A DISGRACE! WHAT UTTER INEPTITUDE!
TO THINK THAT I, THE WARDEN ENTRUSTED WITH THE FOUR NORTHERN DOMAINS...
AUGH...
...HAVE ALLOWED THOSE MERE INSECTS TO INFEST HIS GRACE'S LANDS FOR AN ENTIRE MONTH...!
GAN (SLAM)
M-MILORD!?
GAN
GAN
GAN
GAN
GAN
GAN
GAN
O-ONE THOUSAND APOLOGIES, YOUR GRAAACE!
H-HOW CAN I EVER ATONE FOR THIS......?
GAN
GAN
AAAAAAAAA
AARGH!

......
OSCAR.
Y-
YES?
ビクッ
BIKU
(JOLT)
BRING THE "RAGE SOLEIL" FROM MY BEDCHAMBER TO ME...
Y-YOU DON'T MEAN TO USE THE TREASURE SPEAR NOW, DO YOU...!?

I SAID TO BRING IT HERE. ARE YOU DEAF?
YOU DAMN SCUUUU-UUUM !!!!
A-AT ONCE!
ダッ DA (DASH)
ダッ DA
ダッ DA
BA (BAM)

OUT OF MY WAY!
GYAAH!
DOKA (WHAM)
I WAS A FOOL TO LEAVE MATTERS IN ALL OF YOUR HANDS!
JYUUUU (SIZZLE)
DA (STOMP)
DA
DA
THERE ARE WORTH-LESS, PARA-SITIC, POISON-OUS INSECTS IN THE EMPIRE ...!
BRIGANDS WHO RAVAGE HIS GRACE'S LAND, FREY-JAGARD—
I CANNOT... ALLOW IT!
AS SUCH, I CALL UPON THE TREASURE SPEAR TO FEED OFF MY RAGE!

GOOOOO (FWOOM)
OOOOO (WHOOSH)
THEY WILL LEARN JUST HOW HOT MY INNER WRATH BURNS!!

RAGE SOLEIL !!
DO (SHOOM)

HIGH SCHOOL
PRODIGIES HAVE
IT EASY EVEN IN
ANOTHER
WORLD!

CHARACTER FILE 09

Oslo el Gustav

The Warden of the North who oversees the four northern domains, including Findolph. He is also a Platinum Knight whose powerful spells make him an Imperial Prime Mage. Known as the Fastidious Duke, he has pledged his absolute, undying loyalty to the emperor.

AWAKEN...
...PLEASE ......
DANGER......
DANGER ENCROACHES...... UPON THE SEVEN HEROES...
YOUR POWER...IS NEEDED......
PLEASE...... LEAD THEM TO SALVATION......

BA (FWIP)
!?
WHAT...... WAS THAT...?
HAAAH!
HAAAH!

AH!
THE SEVEN HEROES...
TSUKASA AND EVERYONE... THEY'RE IN DANGER...

I HAVE TO WARN THEM...!

CHAPTER 25: CRIMSON NIGHT

INDUSTRIAL DISTRICT, DORMUNDT
This is beaaa-aaaary bad!!
KUMA-USA!?
!EMERGENCY!
WARNING
Emergency notifications to all devices have been triggered!
Altitude—6,000 meters!
200 kilometers away!
A projectile is approaching Dormundt from the sky south-southeast at high speed!

Enacting emergency protocols!
...!
KUMAUSA! PREPARE THE AIR DEFENSE COUNTER-ATTACK!
Roger that!

Ringo-kun.
TSU-TSUKASA-SAN...!
I've grasped the situation from the emergency notification.
WHAT DO WE KNOW ABOUT THIS PROJECTILE?
Based on sonar analysis, it appears to be...
...a spear.
From its current trajectory and the angle, we've got an approximate point of origin!
It was launched from Gustav domain!
GOOOOO (SHOOM)
AT THIS RATE, THE SPEAR IS SET TO CRASH...
...R-RIGHT IN THE MIDDLE OF DORMUNDT!
COULD IT PERHAPS BE OSLO EL GUSTAV'S INFAMOUS HEAVENLY FIRE?
THE SPELL THAT RAZED AN ENEMY BASE IN A SINGLE NIGHT ......!?
ZAWA (CLAMOR)
D-DIDN'T YOU SAY THEY WOULDN'T STRIKE UNTIL WINTER'S END!?

DO WHATEVER IT TAKES TO SHOOT DOWN THAT WEAPON, RINGO-KUN.
KUMA-USA! THE AIR DEFENSE COUNTER-ATTACK IS READY, RIGHT!?
Fur sure!
Activating all four anti-aircraft missile pods!
Unit 01, at full blast!!
DO (SHNK)
DO
DO
DO
DOGOOON (KABOOM)

!?
N-no good!
It had no effect at all!?
WHY... NOT...!?
IT MUST BE GUARDED BY MAGIC...
If that missile bear-rage did nothing, that's claws for alarm.

...Ringo-kun, did our counterstrike affect the spear's trajectory at all?
UMM... H-HANG ON...
KATA
KATA (CLACK)
KATA
Yes, a little! Now it's set to crash in the south-east, in the aristocrats' residential district ...!
DORMUNDT
Northwest—Industrial District
Northeast—Residential District (Commoners)
Southwest—Port/Commercial District
Southeast—Residential District (Aristocrats)
SO THE TRAJECTORY WAS ALTERED. USE THE REMAINING MISSILES TO DIVERT THE SPEAR'S LANDING TO OUTSIDE THE CITY.
GUSTAV'S HEAVENLY FIRE IS MORE LIKE AN INCENDIARY STRIKE.
IF IT'S NOT A DIRECT HIT, IT DOESN'T POSE A HUGE THREAT.
KUMAUSA! LET'S KNOCK THE SPEAR'S ANGLE DOWN WITH OUR MISSILES, SO IT LANDS IN THE SEA SOUTHEAST OF THE CITY!
GOT IT!
Roger that!
Unit 02, at full blast!!
DO (SHNK)
DO
DO
DO

Unit 03!
DOGOON (KABOOM)
DO
DO
DO
POINT OF IMPACT WILL NOW BE...THE OUTSKIRTS OF THE DISTRICT!
Unit 04 should pawsitively finish the job.

BIII (BEEP)
I can't bear to see this!
The missile pod in the aristocrats' district won't activate!
The air defense missiles won't launch!
NO WAY!?

ANALOG ERROR ...!?
WHY!? DID SNOW GET IN AND DAMPEN THE CIRCUITRY!?
Oh no!
We're gonna bear the impact in 3, 2...!
GET DOWN !!

GA
(BWOOM)
OOOOO
(BWOOSH)

WHAT WAS THAT FLASH!?
THERE'S A FIRE!
YES, I AM THE KNIGHT ETERNALLY LOYAL TO HIS GRACE.
WHAT IS IT?
HOT! HOT !!
GOOOOOO (FWOOM)
I-IT'S ...
OSLO EL GUSTAV!
OOO (WHOOSH)
IT'S HIIIIM!
ROTTEN VERMIN NOW DEFILE THE EMPEROR'S DIVINE GARDEN.
THEY MUST LEARN THERE IS NO PLACE FOR THEM TO NEST IN THESE LANDS!

THE FLAMES OF MY RAGE ...
...WILL BURN YOU TO YOUR VERY SOULS!
BA (BURST)
RAGE SOLEIL!
ZA (SHOOM)
ZA
EEK ...!
ZA
ZA
EEEEEK!
ZA
GOOOOO
KYAAAAH!!

IT'S DUKE GUSTAV'S HEAVENLY FIRE! WE'RE DONE FOOOR!
GYAAAAAH!
BO (SHOOM)
UWAAAAH!
GOOOO (BWOOSH)

K-KYLE! WHAT ON EARTH IS HAPPENING!?
WAAAAAAA (WAIL)
H-HOW THE HELL SHOULD I KNOW!?
DID I JUST HEAR SOMEONE SAY "GUSTAV"?
DON'T BE A DUMBASS! WHY HERE, WHERE WE NOBLES OF THE REALM LIVE!?
!?
FU (SHADE)

UWAAAAAAH!!
NWAAAH!
DOKA (THWAK)
Y-YOU'RE ......!
YOU OKAY, THERE...
...LI'L IMPERIAL NOBLES?

IS EVERYONE OKAY?
TSUKASA-DONO! WH-WHAT SHOULD WE DO!?
ZAWA (CHATTER)
WE'D BETTER RUN! THE FLAMES WILL REACH HERE BEFORE LONG!
ZAWA
B-BUT THERE ARE STILL RESIDENTS WHO ARE CAUGHT UP IN IT...!

REMAIN CAAALM!

I AM AKATSUKI, GOD OF THE SEVEN LUMINARIES!
LISTEN TO ME, FORMER NOBLES OF THIS DISTRICT!
DORMUNDT HAS BEEN DEALT A BLOW MOST FOUL!
THE EMPIRE WOULD SEE THE ENTIRE CITY DESTROYED, TOGETHER WITH YOU FINE PEOPLE!
NO WAY IN HELL!
ZAWA
YOU LIE... RIGHT!?
BUT PANIC NOT, FOR THE SEVEN LUMINARIES WILL NOT FORSAKE YOU!
OUR TROOPS ARE ON THEIR WAY TO LEAD A SPEEDY EVACUATION!

THOSE OF YOU WITHOUT THE STRENGTH TO FLEE ON YOUR OWN—ALLOW THEM TO LEND YOU A HAND!
WE WILL NOT ABANDON A SINGLE ONE OF YOU!

LET ME REPEAT...
AH!
THAT'S RIGHT! ITEM 3, CLAUSE 2 IN THE EMERGENCY MANUAL!
SO YOU'VE REMEMBERED, THEN.
AT THIS STAGE, I HAVE NO DIRECT ORDERS FOR YOU ALL...
...AS THE MEASURES WE MUST TAKE IN THIS SITUATION ARE DETAILED IN THE MANUAL.

AFTER ALL, ONCE I'VE DEPARTED THIS LAND, YOU WILL CONTINUE TO PROTECT THIS CITY FOR YEARS TO COME.
REMAIN CALM AND COLLECTED...
...AND DO WHAT MUST BE DONE WITH CARE.
IT'LL BE ALL RIGHT.
Y-YES!

THE EMERGENCY MANUAL—
WRITTEN BY NONE OTHER THAN HIGH SCHOOL PRODIGY TSUKASA MIKOGAMI.
IT IS A DETAILED SET OF INSTRUCTIONS FOR CIRCUMSTANCES THAT MIGHT BEFALL DORMUNDT.

—I AM NOT A PROPHET...
...SO I CANNOT ACCURATELY PREDICT THE FUTURE.
HOWEVER, I CAN PROVIDE CONJECTURES ABOUT ANY NUMBER OF SCENARIOS.
AS SUCH, I HAVE DRAFTED COUNTER-MEASURES FOR THOSE FORESEEABLE SITUATIONS.

DORMUNDT MAY FIND ITSELF IN THE FOLLOWING CRISES, WITH VARIOUS POTENTIAL OUTCOMES.
HERE YOU WILL FIND A COMPREHENSIVE GUIDE TO BOTH THESE CRISES AND THE STEPS NECESSARY TO RESOLVE THEM.

THE CITIZENS SEEM TO BE EVACUATING WITHOUT A HITCH.
...HOW-EVER...
...THE FLAMES ARE FIERCER THAN ANTICI-PATED.
AT THIS RATE, THE FIRE MAY SPREAD TO THE NEIGHBORING DISTRICTS.

BUT WE CAN'T ALLOW THE CITY TO BE CONSUMED—
NOT WHEN IT REPRESENTS THE BIRTH AND BUDDING OF EQUALITY IN THIS WORLD.
TENS OF BILLIONS OF FUTURE LIVES ARE DEPENDING ON OUR SUCCESS HERE...
...HEY. IT'S ME.

Tsukasa
Incoming Call
HOW'RE THINGS ON YOUR END?
No issues.
ONCE THE CITIZENS HAVE EVACUATED AS PER THE MANUAL, WE'LL TAKE ACTION.
ARE THE PREPA-RATIONS COMPLETE?
RIGHT ON TARGET FOR THAT THING WE TALKED ABOUT.

READY TO DO IT WHENEVER.

HIGH SCHOOL
PRODIGIES HAVE
IT EASY EVEN IN
ANOTHER
WORLD!

ZEST BERNARD ...!
THE TRAITOROUS KNIGHT WHO TURNED HIS BACK ON THE EMPIRE...
WHY'D YOU SAVE AN IMPERIAL NOBLE LIKE ME!?
THE EMPIRE'S S'POSED TO LOOK AFTER ITS NOBLES IN A CRISIS—
YOU MIGHT BE CONVINCED OF THAT, BUT...
...THE FASTIDIOUS DUKE OSLO EL GUSTAV AIN'T SUCH A CARING GUY.
HE'S GOT NO SYMPATHY FOR NOBLES WHO CAN'T DEFEND THEIR DOMAIN.
THIS NIGHTMARE WE'RE SEEING'S PROOF OF THAT.
RGH ......!

IN THIS DAMNED EMPIRE THAT OPERATES ON SURVIVAL OF THE FITTEST...
...THERE AIN'T MUCH DIFFERENCE BETWEEN COMMONERS AND NOBLES AT THE END OF THE DAY.
PEOPLE WITH POWER EXPLOIT THOSE BELOW 'EM AND EXTERMINATE 'EM LIKE PESTS WHEN IT'S CONVENIENT.
SURE, OF COURSE! THAT'S THE GOLDEN RULE IN OUR EMPIRE!

......OH YEAH? THEN GO THROW YOURSELF INTO DUKE GUSTAV'S FIRES OF RAGE, WHY DON'CHA?
IF YOU NOBLES'RE ALL ABOUT PRESERVING THAT IMPERIAL ORDER, IT'S BASICALLY YOUR DUTY.
THE SEVEN LUMINARIES, THOUGH... THEY'RE OUT TO CREATE A WORLD WHERE CLASS AND BLOODLINES DON'T MEAN SQUAT.
LEAVING BEHIND A WORLD LIKE THAT FOR MY DAUGHTER? NOW THAT'S A DREAM WORTH DYING FOR.
B-BUT......

THAT'S EXACTLY WHY I TOOK ON THE ROLE OF COMMANDER FOR THE ORDER OF THE SEVEN LUMINARIES.
THE LUMINARIES WANNA SHOW ALL OF US A NEW WORLD.
......

I IMAGINE THE IDEA OF RELINQUISHING YOUR POWER IS UNTHINKABLE TO THE LOT OF YOU...
...BUT THERE'S A WHOLE HOST OF FOLKS STARTING TO SEE FOR THE FIRST TIME HOW A SOCIETY WITH EQUALITY MIGHT ACTUALLY LOOK.
DO ME A FAVOR... AND DON'T FORGET THAT.

NOBODY ASKED YOU FOR HELP! C'MON, MEN!
DA (DASH)

TSU-KASA-DONO!
ALL SURVIVING CITIZENS HAVE FLED THE AREA!
Excellent work.
WITH THE EVACUATION COMPLETE, TRIGGER THE EXPLOSIVES.
Got it.

DOOOON (BOOM)

CHAPTER 26: GLIMMER OF HOPE

TH-THAT EXPLOSION... DON'T TELL ME...
THEY DETONATED THE BOMBS WE GATHERED UP!?

I GET IT.
THEY'RE HOPING TO CONTAIN THE CONFLAGRATION BY WIDENING THE MAIN STREETS.
THE FIRES WILL NOT BE EXTINGUISHED BY WATER ALONE, SO THIS WAS OUR ONLY COURSE OF ACTION, THAT IT WAS.
MASATO-DONO, IT IS IMPRESSIVE FOR YOU TO HAVE AMASSED SUCH A STOCK OF GUNPOWDER, THAT IT IS. NOT THROUGH ORDINARY TRADING, I SUSPECT?
I DIDN'T DO A THING.

SEEMS LIKE GOOD OL' SAINT NICK CROSSED THE WINTERY SEAS TO GIVE US A GIFT.
WE OUGHT TO BE APPRE-CIATIVE, THEN.
SANTA EXISTS IN THIS WORLD? A PLEASANT SURPRISE, THAT IT IS!
NOT... ENOUGH...
TA (TMP)
WHAT HAPPENED, LYRULE-CHAN? WHY'RE YOU DRENCHED IN SWEAT!?
DID YOU GET BURNED OR SOME-THING!?
...WIDENING THE STREETS... ISN'T ENOUGH ...!
IT'S NOT ENOUGH... TO STOP RAGE SOLEIL ...!

WH-WHAT'S THAT MEAN... LYRULE-CHAN ...?
HAAH!
HAAH!
THINK YOUR-SELVES CLEVER, DO YOU?
YOUR PETTY TRICKS WON'T SAVE YOU FROM MY RAAAGE!
BA (BURST)
ZURU (SLIDE)
WHAT THE HELL ...?
GOOOO (BWOOSH)
UWAAAAAH!

HEH HEH... FWAH HA HA HA HA HAAA!!
TREMBLE IN FEAR BEFORE ME! THIS IS THE MIGHT OF MY LOYALTY!
BECOME ONE WITH MY RAGE SOLEIL!
ONCE SET IN MOTION, MY MAGIC BLAZE WILL SCORCH THE EARTH AND SPREAD THROUGHOUT THE LAND WITHOUT END!
THERE'S NO PLACE ON THIS ENTIRE CONTINENT FOR YOU TO FLEE TO!
DIE! DIE! ATONE WITH YOUR LIVES!
ATONE FOR THE GRIEVOUS SIN OF PERMITTING HIS GRACE'S HOLY LANDS TO BE DEFIIIILED!!

WAAAAAAA (WAIL)
RUUUUUUN!
SHOULD'VE KNOWN THERE'S NO HOPE OF ACTUALLY BEATING THE EMPIRE!

THIS CHAOS WON'T CEASE UNTIL THE FIRES ARE EXTIN-GUISHED.
NO CHOICE, THEN ...!
AAAA (HOWL)
ATTENTION, ALL PERSONNEL! WE'RE SHIFTING PHASES. ENACT ITEM 3, CLAUSE 4 OF THE EMERGENCY MANUAL.
EVACUATE THE ENTIRE CITY...!
GIRI (GRIP)
......

WE'RE... ABANDONING DORMUNDT!

TSU-KASA-SAN!
THANK GOODNESS YOU'RE SAFE, LYRULE-KUN... YOU NEED TO FLEE AT ONCE—
THAT'S NOT NECESSARY!
THERE'S A WAY TO BREAK RAGE SOLEIL!
......YOU TRULY KNOW HOW TO DEFEAT THIS MAGIC?
YES!

RAGE SOLEIL IS WARCRAFT MAGIC.
THAT IS, IT'S A KIND OF MAGIC THAT TAKES YEARS TO MOLD INTO FORM.
IT BINDS "BLAZE SPIRITS" TO THE CURSED CORE OF THAT SPEAR!
THE FIRE WILL PURSUE US AS FAR AS WE RUN, UNLESS WE BREAK THE SPEAR ITSELF!
THAT MEANS, BY DESTROYING THE SPEAR, WE CAN PUT A STOP TO THE DESTRUCTION!!
HOW D'YOU KNOW ALL THIS, LYRULE-CHAN...?
I DON'T KNOW HOW I KNOW...
BUT...... EVEN THOUGH I DON'T KNOW, I KNOW ...!

THE INSTANT I SET EYES ON THOSE FLAMES, I KNEW WHAT KIND OF MAGIC IT WAS.
EVERY DETAIL JUST POPPED INTO MY HEAD...
...LIKE IT WAS SOMETHING I KNEW BEFORE I WAS EVEN BORN...!
PLEASE BELIEVE ME!

OKAY... I'LL BELIEVE YOU.

All those missiles bearly scratched it, you know.
This'll be beary tricky.
THAT LEAVES US WITH THE PROBLEM OF HOW TO DESTROY THE SPEAR... IT'LL BE A CHALLENGE, FOR SURE.
HUH ...?
ANY IDEAS POPPIN' INTO YOUR HEAD ABOUT THAT, LYRULE-CHAN?
......YOU ALL... REALLY BELIEVE ME...?
OF COURSE WE DO.
THIS CHANGE IN YOU CLEARLY HAS YOU FLUSTERED AND SCARED, YET...
...YOU STILL CHARGED OUT HERE TO HELP EVERYONE.

I HAVE NO REASON TO DOUBT SUCH COURAGE.
NGH—!
GUI (WIPE)
...YOU DON'T NEED ANY SPECIAL ABILITY TO BREAK THE SPEAR.
A SIMPLE, STRONG IMPACT SHOULD BE ENOUGH TO CRACK IT.

B-but our missiles couldn't even dent it!
THAT WAS BEFORE RAGE SOLEIL TRULY ACTIVATED, WHEN THE CONCENTRATION OF THE BLAZE SPIRITS MADE IT IMPENETRABLE.
HOWEVER, NOW THAT THE BLAZE SPIRITS ARE SPREADING ACROSS THE CITY...
...EVEN THAT EARLIER ATTACK COULD GET THE JOB DONE.

DO WE HAVE ANY MISSILES LEFT, RINGO-KUN?
J-JUST THE ONE LOADED ONTO KUMAUSA.
...BUT...

...THE SPEAR'S PLANTED IN THE GROUND... OUT OF RANGE OF OUR AIR DEFENSE RADAR.
PLUS, ALL THE FIRE IS CREATING A LOT OF AIR TURBULENCE...
GUIDING THE MISSILE IN...WOULD PROBABLY BE NEAR IMPOSSIBLE.
WHY DON'T WE HAVE KUMAUSA BRING IT RIGHT UP TO THE SPEAR?
No way!
Those high temperatures would melt my circuits...

THEN ALLOW ME TO GO FORTH.
WHADDAYA MEAN BY THAT, AOI-CHAN?

KUMAUSA-DONO WILL LAUNCH THE MISSILE, AND I SHALL GUIDE IT TO THE TARGET MANUALLY.
WHAAAT!?

I MUST SAY THAT SOUNDS... AWFULLY RECKLESS...

WITH ALL DUE RESPECT, TSUKASA-DONO...
...I SHAN'T ALLOW YOU TO MAKE LIGHT OF MY ABILITIES.

HIGH SCHOOL PRODIGIES HAVE IT EASY EVEN IN ANOTHER WORLD!

CHARACTER FILE 10

Zest Bernard

Former Silver Knight and Captain of the Dormundt Guard. He now serves as Commander of the Order of the Seven Luminaries. Adores his daughter Airi.

I AM A MARTIAL ARTIST HERALDED AS A PRODIGY THE WORLD OVER.
ONLY I CAN COMPREHEND MY OWN LIMITS, WHICH THE REST OF YOU CANNOT EVEN IMAGINE.
THEREFORE, HOWEVER IMPLAUSIBLE IT MAY SEEM TO YOU, TSUKASA-DONO...
...I AM CAPABLE OF ALL THAT I CLAIM, THAT I AM.
—VERY WELL.
I HAVE FAITH...
...IN OUR PRODIGIOUS SWORD MASTER, AOI ICHIJOU.

CHAPTER 27: DEMONSTRATION OF SKILL

HEAVE-HO!
RINGO-DONO! I AM PREPARED, THAT I AM!

ZA (SHHF)

KATA
KATA (CLACK)
KATA
GAN (SHNK)
Paw-sitively ready!
AOI-KUN, WE'RE RELYING ON YOU TO ESCORT THAT MISSILE!
AND THAT I SHALL!
Launching missile—!

DOON
(SHOOM)

DO
DO
DO
DO
(RUMBLE)
LIVE

THAT'S NUTS! SHE'S ACTUALLY RUNNING ALONGSIDE THE MISSILE...
AT THIS RATE, DON'CHA THINK SHE'LL REACH THE TARGET IN NO TIME FLAT?

...NO.
I'M AFRAID IT WON'T BE THAT SIMPLE.

GOOO
(FWOOM)
NWAAAH!
GA
GA
GA
GA
(DMM)
GA
GA
YAH!!
GUIN
(YANK)
DO
DO
DO
DO
DO

INCREDIBLE... BUT AHEAD, THERE'S...
...A DEAD-END.
OH NO! SHE'S GOT NOWHERE TO RUN!
AOI-KUN...!
GA (DMM)
GA
GA
GA
GA
GA
GA
NOW RIIIISE !!

GOOOOO
(FWOOSH)
MERELY ASCENDING EVER HIGHER WON'T GET ME ANYWHERE, THAT IT WON'T.
GYUMU
(SQUISH)
PUSUN
(SPUTTER)
HNGH!
GURUN
(SPIN)
THE SPEAR IS IN SIGHT.

GOOOOOOO (FWOOOM)
YOU CUNNING LITTLE FLY...!
YOU WON'T LET ME PAST SO EASILY, I SUPPOSE?
FALL TO YOUR DOOM!
BUN (BURST)
KUH!
BO (SHOOM)

FALL,
FALL,
FAAAAA-
AAALL!!
GOOOOO

WHERE HAVE YOU GOOONE !?
PESKY LITTLE FLYYY —!!
GA
GA (DMM)
GA
GA
GA
HYUN (ZOOM)

GOOOO
(SHOOOM)

RINGO-
DONOO-
OOO!!
LOCKED
ONTO THE
TARGET!
NOT
ON MY
WAAAA-
AATCH!!
PAN
(SMACK)

BA
(BURST)
With her bear hands—!?
WHAT—!?
HEAVEN'S ULTIMATE...

GOOO (SHWOOM)
...DEW BREEZE BLADE!
GAAAAAAAAAAAH!
I DID TELL YOU, THAT I DID.
WHAT I CLAIM TO BE CAPABLE OF...
...IS WELL WITHIN THE REALM OF POSSIBILITY.

DOGOOOON (KABOOM)
IMPOS-SIBLE ...!
HOW CAN THIS BEEEEE !?

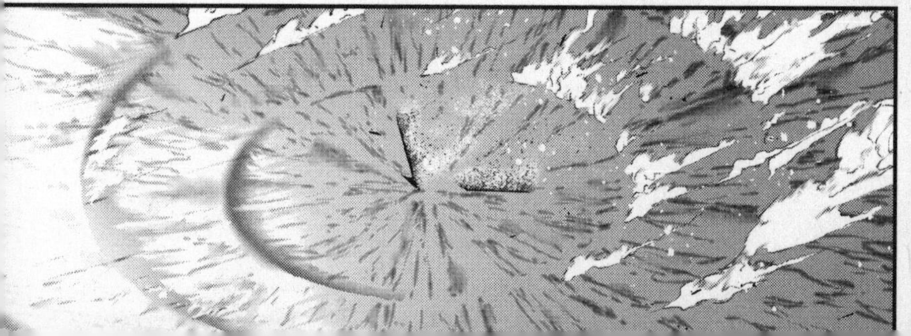

AOI-CHAN'S THE ABSOLUTE GREATEST!!
HONESTLY... THAT GIRL ONLY KNOWS HOW TO OVERDO IT.

L-LOOK! THE... FLAMES ......!
THEY'RE GOING OUT...

GUSTAV DOMAIN
GWAAAAAAAH!!
MILORD!
THIS IS UNHEARD OF! HOW COULD MY RAGE SOLEIL BE BROKEN ...!?

GOING BY HER GARB AND SWORD...
...SHE'S AN AGENT OF YAMATO, NO DOUBT ...!
AND YET...
BOTA (GUSH)
BOTA

...THAT FLYING SHELL SPITTING FLAMES... I'VE NEVER SEEN ANYTHING LIKE IT.
THESE NORTH-ERN REBELS HAVE A POWER EVEN THE YAMATO IMPERIAL ARMY DID NOT POS-SESS.

THESE ARE NO ORDINARY PESTS WHO'VE MADE THEIR NEST IN THE NORTH.

UWAAAAAH!
GOOOO (FWOOM)
OSCAR! ROUND UP EVERY LAST SOLDIER IN THIS DOMAIN AND HAVE THEM ASSEMBLE IN THE CAPITAL.
YES, SIR!
WHAT ARE KNIGHTS, IF THEY DON'T PROTECT THEIR LAND... AND THEIR BETTERS!?
THIS DIRE A THREAT TO HIS GRACE CANNOT BE IGNORED.

THE FULL MIGHT OF OUR FORCES WILL MARCH UPON FINDOLPH!
WE WILL LEAVE NARY A SINGLE ANT ALIVE IN OUR WAKE!!

HIGH SCHOOL
PRODIGIES HAVE
IT EASY EVEN IN
ANOTHER
WORLD!

CHARACTER FILE 11

Elm Villagers

When the high school prodigies crash-landed from another world, the villagers nursed them back to health and looked after them. While the prodigies are off fighting battles, Winona, her father Ulgar, and the others are always ready to welcome them back.

WHAT... WILL BECOME OF US?
DON'T ASK ME!
EVEN THOUGH WE NOBLES WERE STILL IN THE CITY...
...I CAN'T BELIEVE THE EMPIRE WOULD DO A CRAZY THING LIKE THIS...

HEY, WEE NOBLES OVER THERE.

WE GOT SOME FIRES GOIN' AND FOOD COOKIN' YONDER, SO C'MON OVER.
YOU'LL ALL CATCH COLDS, DRESSED AS YOU ARE.
HERE! BLANKETS!
......GIVING CHARITY TO NOBLES? YOU MUST BE ENJOYING THIS, HUH?
WAIT! KYLE!?
WE ARE IN NO PLACE TO BE SAYING SUCH THINGS ...!

IT MUST BE SO FUN FOR YOU RABBLE TO SEE US LIKE THIS!
DAMN HYPOCRITES!
......FOR FOLKS WHO DO NONE OF THE WORK, YOU NOBLES SURE THROW YOUR WEIGHT AROUND.
GIVEN YOU ALL LOOK DOWN ON US, IF YOU WERE TO ASK IF I LIKE YOU OR NOT—
I HATE YOU, Y'KNOW.

THERE, SEE! SO WHY REACH OUT TO—
BUT...
...THERE'S NO DIFFERENCE BETWEEN RICH AND POOR WHEN IT COMES TO THE BITING COLD NIGHT AIR OR TO EMPTY BELLIES.
FUWA (FLAP)

WE'RE ALL JUST PEOPLE, AND WE KNOW DARN WELL HOW TOUGH LIFE CAN BE.
...WE'RE NOT ABOUT TO LEAVE YOU BOYS IN THE LURCH.
?!

C'MON... IF YOU UNDERSTAND, THEN GET YOUR BUTTS OVER HERE.
GIMME ANY MORE LIP, AND I'LL HAVE TO DRAG YOU ALONG!

.........I'M SORRY...

CHAPTER 28: A BATTLE IGNITED

WITH THE SPEAR BROKEN, THE BLAZE SPIRITS HAVE BEEN RELEASED FROM THE CURSE.
THEY WON'T BE BURNING UP THE CITY ANY LONGER.
AND THEY'RE THANKING US ALL...
YOU CAN HEAR THE SPIRITS' VOICES, LYRULE-KUN?
YES. I WAS ABLE TO HEAR THE BLAZE SPIRITS SCREAMING OUT.
THEY WERE SAYING "HELP US," "WE DON'T WANT TO DO THIS," AND SO ON.
THEIR VOICES WERE FULL OF GRIEF.

BUT... THEY'LL BE OKAY NOW.
WE OWE YOU OUR THANKS AS WELL, LYRULE-KUN.
YOUR BRAVERY IS WHAT SAVED THE REMAINDER OF THE CITY.

THANK YOU.

......BUT THERE WERE SO MANY PEOPLE... WE WERE UNABLE TO SAVE.

THIS DISASTER... IS THE RESULT OF WHAT WE STARTED, ISN'T IT?

WHEN I DECLARED WAR TO STEAL LYRULE-KUN BACK FROM THAT DESPOT...
...IT PAINED HER TO KNOW EVERYONE MADE SACRIFICES FOR HER SAKE.
I WONDER IF SHE'S SUFFERING BECAUSE SHE FEELS THE SACRIFICES MADE HERE ARE HER DOING AS WELL...
LYRULE-KUN'S AN ORPHAN HERSELF.
SHE LIKELY FEELS RESPONSIBLE FOR THE CHILDREN WHO LOST THEIR PARENTS TONIGHT.
BUT THIS IS A BATTLE THE PEOPLE CHOSE TO FIGHT.
IT'S NOT A BURDEN LYRULE-KUN NEEDS TO BEAR ALONE...
IF YOU'RE REGRETTING US STARTING THIS WAR...
...YOUR LINE OF THINKING IS OFF BASE.

THIS PEOPLE'S REVOLUTION REPRESENTS A TURNING POINT IN HISTORY.
ONCE BEGUN, EVEN IF IT MEANS MAKING COUNTLESS SACRIFICES...
...IT IS IMPERATIVE WE SEE IT THROUGH...
NATURALLY, THERE'S NO FUTURE FOR A NATION THAT SLAUGHTERS ITS OWN CITIZENRY WITHOUT MERCY.

SO ALL WE CAN DO IS ASK FORGIVENESS FROM THOSE WHO GAVE THEIR LIVES.
TO SAVE TENS OF THOUSANDS OF FUTURE LIVES, AND TO PREVENT THEIR SACRIFICES FROM BEING IN VAIN—
THAT ALONE IS WHY WE MUST SEE THIS WAR THROUGH TO ITS END.
......YES!

TSU-KASA-SAN.
BEFORE... ALL THIS UPROAR, I HEARD A VOICE SPEAK TO ME IN A DREAM.
A WOMAN'S VOICE SAID, "PLEASE LEAD THE SEVEN HEROES TO SALVATION"!
AFTER HEARING IT, MAGIC KNOWLEDGE SUDDENLY WELLED UP IN MY MIND...
...AND THE SPIRITS' VOICES BEGAN TO FILL MY EARS.
THE TIMING IS TOO COINCIDENTAL TO WRITE IT OFF AS JUST AN ODD DREAM.

THERE MUST BE A HIDDEN CONNECTION BETWEEN YOU, LYRULE-KUN...
...AND THE MYSTERY WOMAN, AND THE REASON WE'RE IN THIS WORLD.
AND IT SEEMS LIKE THE VOICE IS MAINLY TRYING TO HELP YOU.
YES... I THINK SO TOO.

I DON'T KNOW WHO'S SPEAKING TO ME...OR WHY I CAN HEAR THESE VOICES, BUT...
...SHE TALKED ABOUT MY "POWER," WHICH MUST BE KNOWLEDGE OF MAGIC AND THE ABILITY TO HEAR SPIRITS.
SO...

...I'M GOING TO START STUDYING MAGIC!
PERHAPS I'LL EVEN DISCOVER A WAY TO HELP YOU SEVEN GET BACK TO YOUR WORLD!

......
RIGHT.
WE'RE LUCKY TO HAVE YOU ON OUR SIDE.

NO WAAAAY!!
KIIIN (SHRILL)
LOWER YOUR VOICE, SHINOBU.
You're kidding! Rage Soleil seriously went your way already!?
Yes.
I-IS EVERYONE OKAY!? THAT'S S'POSED TO BE SOME REAL NASTY MAGIC!
Somehow, only about a third of the city suffered major damage.
ARRRGH!
H-HOW HUMILIATING! THIS IS THE THIRD MOST HUMILIATING THING THAT'S HAPPENED IN MY LIFE!
I'M ALWAYS S'POSED TO GET THE SCOOP ON DIRTY DEALINGS BEFORE THEY GO LIVE...
...BUT HE GOT THE JUMP ON MEEEE!

THE BASTARD FIRED HIS SHOT BEFORE EVEN LINKING UP WITH HIS ARMY ...?
HOPE HE GOES BALD!
STUPID GUSTAV DOESN'T KNOW THE MEANING OF PATIENCE, HUH!?
GUGI (CLENCH)
GI
We've already dealt with Rage Soleil, though.

That aside... good work making contact with the resistance... the Blue Brigade.
THAT, OF COURSE, INCLUDES INTEL ON THE BLUE BRIGADE ITSELF.
Mm... Got it. I'll text you an update later.
I HAVEN'T DECIDED TO TEAM UP WITH THEM JUST YET, YOU SEE.
You and Elch should continue working with them while feeding the rest of us intel.
HAAAAH...
I'M REALLY SORRY...
SHUN (DROOP)

WAS THAT SHINOBU?
YES. CALLING TO TELL US HOW TO HANDLE RAGE SOLEIL...
SHE WAS FRUSTRATED AT BEING A STEP BEHIND.
WELL, SURE. IT DISGRACES HER GOOD NAME AS A TOP JOURNALIST.

SO WHAT'S THIS OTHER PLAN YOU MENTIONED ANYWAY?
......OH, ABOUT THAT...

I HEAR MAGIC INTENSITY IS PRO-PORTIONAL TO THE NUMBER OF SPIRITS AT WORK.
THE GREATER THE NUMBER OF WIND SPIRITS IMBUED IN A WIND BLADE, THE BETTER IT CUTS.
AS FOR THAT WARCRAFT MAGIC, A SINGLE MISSILE WAS ENOUGH TO TAKE IT OUT ONCE ITS BLAZE SPREAD.
THIS IS ALL BASICALLY WHAT LYRULE-KUN ALREADY TOLD US.
IT'S STILL JUST A HUNCH, BUT...
SOUNDS SPOT-ON TO ME.

MAGIC OR NOT, THERE'S PLENTY TO LEARN THROUGH RESEARCH
THAT'S WHAT I BASED THIS CONJECTURE ON.
......
I SEE.

EVEN WITHOUT LYRULE-CHAN'S ADVICE...
...HE WAS ALREADY PREPARED TO COUNTER UNKNOWN FORCES LIKE MAGIC...?
!
!
WHAT A GUY.

YOU'RE THE ONLY ONE IN THE WORLD... WHO I CAN TRULY RELY ON, MAN.
THAT'S EXACTLY WHY...

...THIS GUY, WHO'S TRYING TO SAVE EVERYONE...
...AND ME, WHO'S TRYING TO GET MY HANDS ON EVERYTHING I CAN...
...ARE GONNA GO OUR SEPARATE WAYS SOMEDAY.

BY THE WAY, MERCHANT, THERE'S THE URGENT MATTER...
...OF DORMUNDT'S FOOD AND SUPPLIES THAT WERE LOST TO THE FIRE...
THAT. RIGHT.
PASA (FLAP)

THANKS TO THESE INVENTORIES YOU HAD US COMPILE IN ADVANCE...
...THE CITY'S RE-CONSTRUCTION SHOULD GO SMOOTHLY.
BUT LOSING THOSE FOOD STORES IS GONNA HURT FOR SURE.

EVEN WITH CONTRIBUTIONS FROM NEARBY VILLAGES, WE'RE GONNA RUN DRY IN ABOUT A MONTH.
AND RIGHT WHEN WINTER'S AT ITS COLDEST AND NASTIEST ...

I THOUGHT THAT MIGHT BE THE CASE.
SO WHAT SHOULD WE DO?

ZA (STOMP)
ZA
ZA

THAT'S WHAT WE'RE GOING TO DO—
ZA

TSUKASA-DONO, THE FIRST SQUADRON'S ARMAMENT HAS BEEN FULLY MODERNIZED.
WE'RE FIFTY IN TOTAL, AT YOUR CALL.
ZA

...HEY, HEY! WHAT'S UP YOUR SLEEVE NOW?
I SHOULDN'T NEED TO TELL A TREMENDOUS BUSINESSMAN THIS, BUT...
..."PATIENCE" IS AN INDISPENSABLE QUALITY FOR ANYONE HOPING TO MANAGE PERSONNEL OR CAPITAL.

GUSTAV IS THE KIND OF MAN WHO FIRES OFF HIS ONETIME RAGE SOLEIL WITHOUT WAITING TO MOBILIZE HIS ARMY.
HE'S NOT THE TYPE TO HANG BACK UNTIL THE SNOWS MELT.
IN FACT, I EXPECT HE'S ALREADY ORDERED THE IMPERIAL ARMY TO MOVE OUT.

AND THOSE TROOPS WON'T HAVE A CHOICE BUT TO OBLIGE WHEN THEY'RE GETTING ORDERS FROM GUSTAV, WARDEN OF THE NORTH.
THEY WERE EXPECTING TO INVADE IN SPRING. SO, IN THAT SAME LIGHT EQUIPMENT...
...THEY'LL BE BRAVING THE BLIZZARDS OF THE LE LUK MOUNTAINS IN WINTER. IT'S A SUICIDE MARCH.

WE COULDN'T HAVE ASKED FOR A BETTER CHANCE.
WE'VE NO NEED TO SIT BACK AND WAIT FOR THE ENEMY TO CROSS THE RANGE.
WE'LL MEET THE SUBJUGATING ARMY IN THE MOUNTAINS AND ANNIHILATE THEM.
THE THREE NORTHERN DOMAINS WILL BE UNDER OUR CONTROL BEFORE SPRING.

THERE-AFTER, WITH STILL MORE TERRITORY IN HAND...
...WE WILL FURTHER ESTABLISH OUR DEMOCRATIC NATION.

HIGH SCHOOL PRODIGIES HAVE IT EASY EVEN IN ANOTHER WORLD!

CHARACTER FILE 12

Blue Brigade

Led by Count Blumheart, a classmate of Gustav's at the empire's military academy in their younger days. However, the two are polar opposites when it comes to governance. With the welfare of the citizenry in mind, Blumheart went on to found the Blue Brigade.

BUCHWALD DOMAIN CHECKPOINT, LE LUK MOUNTAIN RANGE
FINDOLPH DOMAIN
CHECK-POINT
BUCHWALD DOMAIN
YEESH, IT'S COLD. ANOTHER BLIZZARD TODAY, HUH?
HEY, SHIFT CHANGE.
'PRECIATE IT. THE POST'S ALL YOURS.
IN THE MEANTIME, I'M GONNA SNEAK SOME BOOZE FROM THE LARDERS ON MY WAY OUT.
WHOA, YOU COULD LOSE YOUR HEAD FOR THAT.
IT'S BASICALLY JUST COLD STORAGE FOR ALL THAT EXTRA FOOD. NOBODY'LL KNOW.
WELL, YOU DON'T WANNA GO TO SLEEP COLD. THAT COULD KILL YOU TOO...
ON THAT NOTE—
DOGOON (KABOOM)
WH- WHAT THEEE —!?

CHAPTER 29: TWO WARS

A... A HOLE THROUGH THE WALL!?
WHO THE HELL'S GOT A CANNON CAPABLE OF BLASTING AWAY MASONRY!?
GWAH!?
PAAN (BANG)
PAAN
GUNFIRE! WE'RE UNDER ATTACK!
R-RIDICULOUS! NOBODY COULD FIRE A GUN IN THIS BLIZZARD—
PAAN
GYAAH!
EEEK!
WAAAH!

AN ENEMY ATTAAACK ...!
GYAAAAH!
GAH !?
DON'T JUST STAND AROUND! START FIGHTING BACK!
SAY THAT ALL YOU WANT, BUT THERE'S NO VISIBILITY IN THIS DARKNESS!
WAAAH!
PAN (BANG)
FLINTLOCKS ARE THE ONLY FIREARMS USABLE IN A SNOWSTORM LIKE THIS.
ON TOP OF THAT, IT'S TOO DARK TO SEE MORE THAN A FEW PACES AWAY.
HOW ARE THEY SNIPING SO ACCURATELY ...!?
EVEN THE TROOPS IN THE IMPERIAL CAPITAL AREN'T ALL EQUIPPED WITH THOSE, SO HOW DID BANDITS GET THEIR HANDS ON THE LATEST TECHNOLOGY ...!?
PAN
GWAH!

WOW...! STILL WISH WE HAD SOME SUNLIGHT, BUT...
...WE CAN TOTALLY SEE THE ENEMY WITH THESE GOGGLES!

AND THESE GUNS—WHOA!
THE SHOT FLIES RIGHT WHERE WE AIM, EVEN WITH ALL THIS WIND.
THE GEAR FROM THOSE ANGELS AIN'T NO JOKE!
SA (SHIFT)
SA

NOW!
BERNARD SQUADRON IS WITH ME!
CHARGE!!
CONRAD SQUADRON! FOCUS YOUR FIRE AT THE TOP OF THE FORTRESS WALL! ANY FOE WHO STANDS UP LOSES HIS HEAD!
TA (CHAK)
TA
TAN
TA
TA
TAN
RAAAAAH!
A WAR CRY!?
DON'T LET THEM IN! SHOOT THEM DEAD!
PAN (BANG)
PAN
UWAH!
GYAAAH!!
DAMN TH—

I-IT'S NO USE! TOO MUCH GUNFIRE TO RISK POKING OUR HEADS OUT!
PAN
PAN
THEY'LL BLOW US AWAY THE SECOND WE STAND!
PAN
PA
PA
PAN
RRRGH!
TO HAVE SUCH A HIGH RATE OF FIRE WITH VIRTUALLY NO PAUSE...
HOW MANY HUNDREDS OF FLINTLOCKS DOES THE ENEMY EVEN HAVE...!!?

WAAAA (PANIC)

THE ENEMY'S ALREADY MADE IT THIS FAR!?
GYAH!
THE WEST WING IS LOST!
LOWER THE IRON GATE!!
GASHAN (CLANG)
COM-MANDER... THE IRON GATE IS—
LEAVE IT TO ME.
BA (FWIP)

DOGOOON (KABOOM)
ALL RIGHT! ONWAAARD !!
...M-MAGIC ...?
YOU IDIOTS! DON'T RETREAT THIS FAR!
MIGHT AS WELL GIVE THEM THIS FORT AS A GIFT!
-EASY OR YOU O SAY.

HOW'RE THEY WIELDING THOSE HUGE IRON SHIELDS AS IF THEY WEIGH NOTHING ...!?
MOVE ASIDE, RANK AND FILE!
BRONZE KNIGHT GAMBINO THE GREAT WILL FIGHT THIS BATTLE FOR YOU!

HAAAAH!
GOO (SHOOM)
DOON (BLAM)

DOSAA (CRASH)
THEY GOT GAMBINO THE GREAT!
THEIR WEAPONS ARE NUTS!
WHO THE HELL ARE THESE PEOPLE!?
WAAAAA (PANIC)

FINDOLPH DOMAIN
CHECKPOINT BETWEEN LE LUK MOUNTAIN RANGE AND BUCHWALD DOMAIN
BERNARD'S FORCES
EAST WING
WEST WING
N
BUCHWALD DOMAIN
JUST AS THE FIGHTING BROKE OUT ON THE FINDOLPH SIDE OF THE CHECKPOINT—
CHECKPOINT SERVICE ENTRANCE, BUCHWALD DOMAIN
KII (CREAK)
HURRY! WE NEED TO GET WORD OF THIS ATTACK TO OUR ALLIES!
ZAKU
ZAKU (CRUNCH)
TAAN (BLAM)
GAH !?
HUH?
TAN
GYAAH!
TA
GAAAH!
TAN

THESE LE LUK BASTARDS NEVER STOOD A CHANCE.
THEY'RE JUST WALTZING INTO OUR LINE OF FIRE.
SHINOBU PINPOINTED A HOLE IN THE CHECKPOINT'S DEFENSES AND FOUND THIS BACK ROUTE.
NO WONDER THE ENEMY DIDN'T SPOT US PASSING BY.
UNTIL BERNARD'S SQUADRON CONQUERS THE CHECK-POINT...
...WE WILL STAY HERE AND SHOOT DOWN THE FLEEING ENEMY!
SO KEEP YOUR WITS ABOUT YOU, EVERYONE!
Y-YES, SIR!!

MILLEVANA, CAPITAL OF GUSTAV DOMAIN
N
DORMIADT
FINDOLPH DOMAIN
CHECKPOINT
LE LUK
BUCHWALD DOMAIN
ARCHRIDE DOMAIN
GUSTAV DOMAIN
MILLEVANA
GUSTAV ASSEMBLED A GOOD TEN THOUSAND TROOPS IN THE CAPITAL TO SUPPRESS THE SEVEN LUMINARIES...
...BUT HIS EFFORTS DIDN'T GET FAR BECAUSE SEVEN THOUSAND OF THOSE SOLDIERS WERE, IN FACT, REBELS WHO TURNED AGAINST HIM AND FOUGHT UNDER THE FLAG OF THE BLUE BRIGADE.
DUE TO THE OVER-WHELMING DISADVANTAGE IN NUMBERS AND THE UNPREPARED-NESS OF GUSTAV'S ARMY...
...THE GOVERNING SEAT WAS SURROUNDED IN A FLASH.
GET DOWN, JEANNE!
DO (THUNK)
DO
DO
DO

YOU REALLY HELPED US OUT BY GETTING YOUR HANDS ON THE CASTLE'S BLUEPRINTS, SHINOBU.
PIIIECE OF CAKE!
WE'RE ALMOST AT THE HEART OF THIS PLACE, JEANNE.
キイ
KII (CREAK)

A SILVER KNIGHT OF THE EMPIRE ...?
YOU BEAR YOUR FANGS AT THE HAND THAT FEEDS YOU!?

THE FOUNDATION OF ANY NATION IS ITS PEOPLE... WITHOUT THEM, THERE IS NO COUNTRY.
AS A NOBLE WHO TYRANNIZES THE PEOPLE, YOU'RE THE REAL TRAITOR HERE, BRINGING HARM TO THE EMPIRE.
DUKE GUSTAV... I'LL GIVE YOU A CHANCE TO SPEAK.

IF YOU HAVE EVEN A BIT OF SENSE LEFT IN YOU...
...SURRENDER NOW AND TURN BACK FROM THIS PATH AS A LOYAL RETAINER!
INTERESTING. SO THE MASTERMIND IS BLUMHEART, IS IT?
THE MAN'S ALWAYS PRATTLED ON ABOUT HOW WE SHOULD NOT DISRESPECT THE CITIZENS...

WHEN WILL YOU FOOLS GIVE UP ON THAT IDIOTIC DREAM?
I, GUSTAV, WILL BURN AWAY THAT MORONIC ILLUSION, ALONG WITH YOUR LIVES!
IF YOU WON'T SURRENDER, YOU LEAVE US NO CHOICE!
COME NOW, SHINOBU!
YOU GOT IT!
BO (FLARE)
BO
BO
BO

FIREBOLT!!
DO (BOOM)

JEANNE, SHIELD YOURSELF!
KA (FLASH)
GWAAAH! MY EYEEES ...!
TRAITOROUS GUSTAV!
YOUR HEAD WILL ROLL!
A LOWLY SILVER LIKE YOU...

...CANNOT MEASURE UP TO A PLATINUM KNIGHT!!
GIIN (SHNNG)
!?
AUGH!!
KAAAAAAAH!!

THE FLASH GRENADE DIDN'T WORK!?
CRAP!!
GOO (BWOOSH)
SA (SHWIP)

HYU (FLICK)
LET'S START WITH A FEINT!!
NWAH!?
GUSA (STAB)
KH—!? HE TOOK THE HIT?
MAYBE RATHER THAN SEEING OUR POSITIONS WITH HIS EYES...
...HE'S SENSING US WITH HEAT!?
IN THAT CASE ...!
HYU
O (WHOOSH)

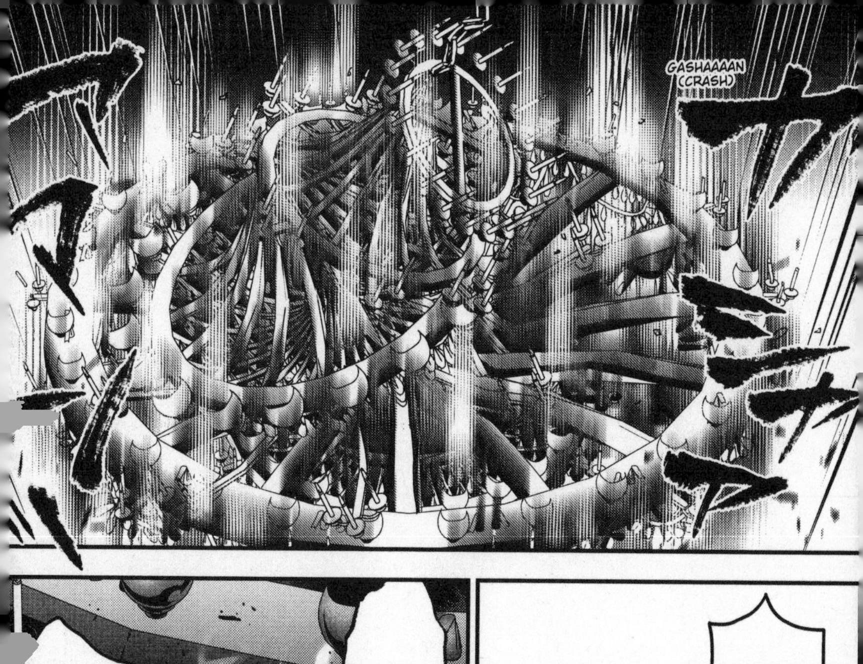
GASHAAAAN
(CRASH)

YOU KILLED HIM!?
OH... MIGHT NOT WANNA ASSUME THAT...

DAMN YOUUU...!
YOU WORMS WHO WOULD DEFY HIS GRACE...!

DON'T GO THINKING YOU'VE DEFEATED THE MIGHTY GUSTAV LIKE THIS!
KA
(FLASH)

OH MAN. THIS GUY REALLY DOES SEEM LIKE BAD NEWS.
JEANNE!
HUH!?
DOGOOOON (KABOOM)

HIGH SCHOOL
PRODIGIES HAVE
IT EASY EVEN IN
ANOTHER
WORLD!

CHARACTER FILE 13

Jeanne du Leblanc

A Silver Knight under Count Blumheart and a member of the Blue Brigade resistance. Though she and high school prodigy Shinobu Sarutobi were at odds at first, the knight saw a potential ally in Shinobu and enlisted her aid.

JEANNE! GRAB ON!
DOGOOOOOON (KABOOM)

DO (RUMBLE)
DO
DO
DO
DO
DO
TH-THIS IS...?

THE GUY MUST'VE PLANTED BOMBS ALL OVER, JUST IN CASE.
OR IT COULD BE MAGIC...
DOON (BOOM)
Y-YOU HAVE MY GRATITUDE, SHINOBU.
I WOULD HAVE BEEN ANNIHILATED.
DOON
AND GOOD WORK, SENSING THAT DANGER.
DANGER-SENSING'S A MUST-HAVE SKILL FOR ANY GOOD JOURNALIST!
HEY!
JEANNE, SOMEONE'S COMING.

AH, THE DRAGOONS ARE THE BLUE BRIGADE'S AERIAL UNITS.
JEANNE, YOU'RE ALL RIGHT!
YES, THANKS TO SHINOBU HERE.
YOU'RE REALLY SOMETHING ELSE! NEVER SAW A PERSON FLY AS WELL AS A DRAGOON WITHOUT THE DRAGON!
EH HEH HEH!

SO WHAT HAPPENED TO OLD GUSTAV!?
IT DOESN'T SEEM LIKE HE COULD HAVE SURVIVED THE BLAST.
THAT'S AMAZING NEWS! BETTER REPORT BACK TO COUNT BLUM-HEART AT ONCE!

BASA (FLAP)
バサッ
...BUT...

...WHAT KIND OF MAN DESTROYS HIMSELF ALONG WITH HIS CASTLE ...?
THAT OLD GUY DIDN'T GIVE A CRAP ABOUT THE LIVES OF OTHERS.
SOMEONE LIKE THAT WOULDN'T HESITATE TO SACRIFICE HIMSELF FOR THE EMPIRE, DON'CHA THINK?
A NATION IS ONLY AS GOOD AS THE PROSPERITY IT PROVIDES ITS PEOPLE.
ONE THAT BOASTS SURVIVAL OF THE FITTEST BY TRAMPLING ALL OVER ITS CITIZENS HAS NO FUTURE AT ALL.
WITH THIS, GUSTAV DOMAIN IS SAVED.
THE GOLD HE HOARDED MUST GO TOWARD HELPING THE PEOPLE REBUILD THEIR LIVES WITHOUT DELAY.
EASIER SAID THAN DONE, IF Y'ASK MEEEE!

CHAPTER 30: ROAD TO REFORM

SOUTHERN RIDGE, LE LUK MOUNTAIN RANGE
THE BUCHWALD/ARCHRIDE JOINT COALITION
ZA (MARCH)
ZA
ZA
FINDOLPH DOMAIN
DORMUNDT
CHECKPOINT
LE LUK
BUCHWALD DOMAIN
ARCHRIDE DOMAIN
GUSTAV DOMAIN
MILLEVANA
ZAKU
ZAKU (CRUNCH)
SO COLD ... CAN'T TAKE IT...
WHAT KINDA IDIOT GIVES ORDERS TO MOBILIZE IN LE LUK AT THIS TIME OF YEAR?
FUCKIN' GUSTAV... SITTING PRETTY IN THE CAPITAL, NOT KNOWING A DAMN THING ABOUT WINTER IN THE MOUNTAINS...
WHY DO WE GOTTA BE OUT HERE TO START WITH?
...SHALL I SHUT THEM UP?
AIDE TO MARQUIS ARCHRIDE GOLDEN KNIGHT KREITZO

LET THEM YAMMER, KREITZO. I FEEL THE SAME WAY THEY DO.
TO THINK GUSTAV WOULD BE SUCH AN IMPATIENT FOOL...
RULER OF ARCHRIDE DOMAIN **MARQUIS ARCHRIDE**

THIS ENEMY IS NO MERE RAGTAG BAND FED UP WITH THE SYSTEM.
THEY WIELD STRANGE POWERS AND EMPLOY RELIGION TO WIN THE PEOPLE OVER.
THEIR POLITICAL VISION HAS EVEN WON NOBLES TO THEIR SIDE, AND THEY'VE ALREADY FORMED WHAT AMOUNTS TO A NATION.

THEY'RE AN ENEMY WITH UNKNOWN ABILITY AND POTENTIAL.
WITHOUT HAVING A GRASP ON THEIR NUMBERS, IT'S CRITICAL TO SEND EVERY LAST SOLDIER TO STAND AGAINST THEM.

THE ORIGINAL STRATEGY WAS TO WAIT FOR SPRING, CONSCRIPT EVERY ABLE-BODIED FIGHTER...
FINDOLPH
LE LUK
BUCHWALD
ARCHRIDE
GUSTAV

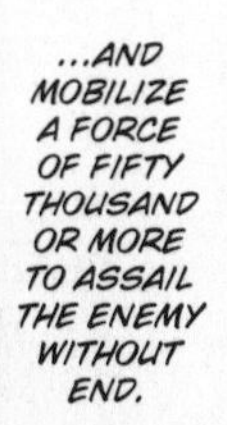
...AND MOBILIZE A FORCE OF FIFTY THOUSAND OR MORE TO ASSAIL THE ENEMY WITHOUT END.

BUT STUBBORN GUSTAV GAVE ORDERS TO MOBILIZE IN WINTER.
AS FOOLISH A LEADER AS THEY COME...
CAMPING OUT IN LE LUK IN THE DEAD OF WINTER IS NEARLY IMPOSSI-BLE...
...SO WE MARCHED TO THE CHECKPOINT IN ONE DAY WITH A MERE THOUSAND MEN—ALL WHO COULD BE ACCOMMODATED.
...AND IN THAT MOMENT, THE PLAN TO MOBILIZE SO FEW WAS DOOMED.

CAN'T EXPECT MUCH FROM FATIGUED TROOPS ON SUCH A RECKLESS MARCH.
UNTIL WE CONVENE WITH GUSTAV'S ARMY, WE'LL JUST GATHER WHAT INTELLIGENCE WE CAN.
IT'S ALL WE SHOULD, AND CAN, DO.

THE CHECK-POINT IS IN SIGHT!
YEAH!
WE FINALLY MADE IT!
BREAK OUT THE MEAT AND BOOZE, QUICK!
GIIII (CREAK)

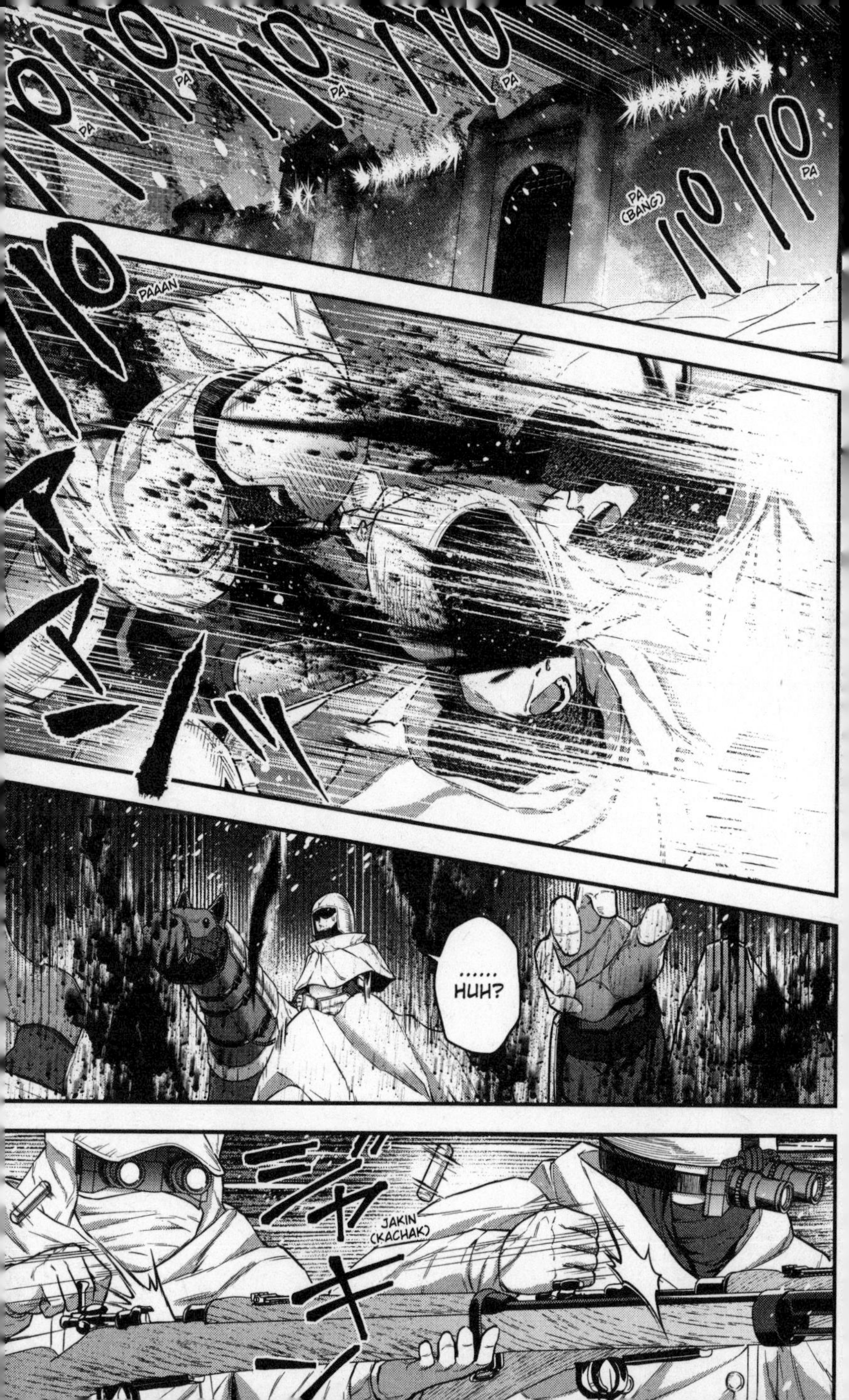
PA
PA
PA
PA
PA
PA (BANG)
PAAAN
......
HUH?
JAKIN (KACHAK)

PA (BANG)
PA
PA
PA
WHAT... IS THIS ...?
PAN
WH- WHAT IN THE WORLD... IS GOING ON—?
GI (PING)
MY LOOORD !!
GI
GI
KREITZO !?
GI
GIN

GYAAAAH!
WH-WHAT THE—!? WHY'RE THE LE LUK GUYS FIRING ON US!?
PAAN
PAN
EEEEK!
AND WHAT'S WITH THESE GUNS!?
PAN

MY LORD! THE CHECKPOINT MUST'VE FALLEN INTO ENEMY HANDS!
GIVE THE ORDER TO FIGHT BACK!
...IT'S NO USE!
THIS MARCH FAILED THE MOMENT THE ENEMY CAPTURED LE LUK!
KREITZO! WATCH MY BACK!
BUOOOOOOO (BWOOOOOOO)
OOOOOO
THAT'S THE SIGNAL TO RETREAT!!
WAAAAAAA (PANIC)
THEY WISED UP QUICK... MAKES SENSE SINCE OLD MARQUIS ARCHRIDE, THE SHREWD GENERAL OF THE NORTH, IS AT THE HELM.

FIRST SQUADRON, WITH ME! WE'RE PURSUING THE ENEMY DOWN THE MOUNTAIN!
ONCE WE REGROUP WITH THE OTHER SQUADRONS, WE'LL INVADE BUCHWALD WITH ALL WE'VE GOT!
NOW MOVE OUT!!
RAAAAAH!
TAN (BLAM)
TAN
TA
TAN

MY LORD! THE ENEMY FIRE IS UNRE-LENTING! WE'RE TAKING HEAVY LOSSES AT THE REAR!
WE'VE NO WAY TO FIGHT BACK! IF THIS KEEPS UP, WE'RE...!
......SO THEY DO MEAN TO PURSUE US.

TELL THE REAR GUARD ARCHRIDE SUFFERED A SNEAK ATTACK AND DIED FROM HIS WOUNDS. THAT'S AN ORDER!
NOW GO!!
WHAT ...!? HUH!?
BUT, MY LORD!! CHAIN OF COMMAND WILL FALL INTO DISARRAY!
EXACTLY. THEY'LL THROW DOWN THEIR ARMS AND RUN FOR IT.
WHA—!?

IT WILL ONLY ENCOURAGE THE ENEMY THAT NOW PURSUES US.
THEY'LL SEE OUR RANKS BREAKING AND GET GREEDY, HOPING TO HUNT DOWN AS MANY OF OURS AS THEY CAN.
THAT GREED PRESENTS US WITH THE CHANCE TO COUNTER.

KREITZO! RIDE AHEAD AND UNITE WITH THE TROOPS IN THE FOOT-HILLS!
YES, SIR!!

WHEN THE ENEMY REACHES THE OPEN FIELD DOWN BELOW, WE MAKE OUR STAND.
PAN (BANG)
ALL THE HANDHELD FIREARMS IN THE WORLD WON'T SAVE THEM ONCE OUR ARMORED CAVALRY CHARGES IN.
IT WOULD BE IMPOSSIBLE TO PUT A DENT IN THOSE BEASTS WITHOUT CANNONS OR POWERFUL MAGIC.
PA
PAN
YOU'LL FALL BEFORE OUR LEGENDARY WARHORSES, THE DREAD MONOKEROS!

ALL CAVALRY!
CHAAAAARGE!!
RAAAAGH!
IT'S LIKE HE'S MAKING THEM DANCE IN THE PALM OF HIS HAND...

LISTEN UP. WHEN WE TAKE THE ENEMY BY SURPRISE IN LE LUK, THEY'LL FLEE AT ONCE, RIGHT?
BUT AS I UNDERSTAND IT, THEY'RE PRETTY SNEAKY THEMSELVES...
...SO THEY'LL PROBABLY LURE US TO AN OPEN FIELD AND SEND THE FULL MIGHT OF THEIR ARMORED CAVALRY AGAINST OUR TROOPS.
SO WE SHOULDN'T PURSUE THEM TOO FAR?
ON THE CONTRARY. THAT'S JUST WHAT WE SHOULD DO.

THE ARMORED CAVALRY IS INDEED A THREAT TO US...
...MAKING THAT UNIT AN IMPORTANT SOURCE OF EMOTIONAL SUPPORT FOR THE ENEMY FORCES.

JUST WHEN THEY THINK THEIR TRUMP CARD HAS WON THEM THE BATTLE...
...WE'LL CRUSH THEM OSTENTATIOUSLY WITH THESE.

PIN (TING)
THE ENEMY WON'T SEE IT COMING.

HYUN (FWISH)
HYUN
THEY'LL SEE US THROWING WHAT APPEAR TO BE STONES AND LAUGH IT OFF.
DO
DO
DO
DO
THEIR GUNS CAN'T SCRATCH US, BUT THESE IMBECILES THINK LITTLE PEBBLES WILL?
THESE REBELS HAVE HAD THEIR FUN!
NOW WE'LL RETURN THE FAVOR AND TRAMPLE EVERY LAST ONE INTO THE DIRT!
DO
DO (RUMBLE)
THUS...
KA (FLASH)

...OUR VICTORY WILL BE ASSURED.
DOON (BOOM)
HUH ...?
...FALL BACK!
ALL TROOPS... RETREAT TO DULLESKOFF ......!

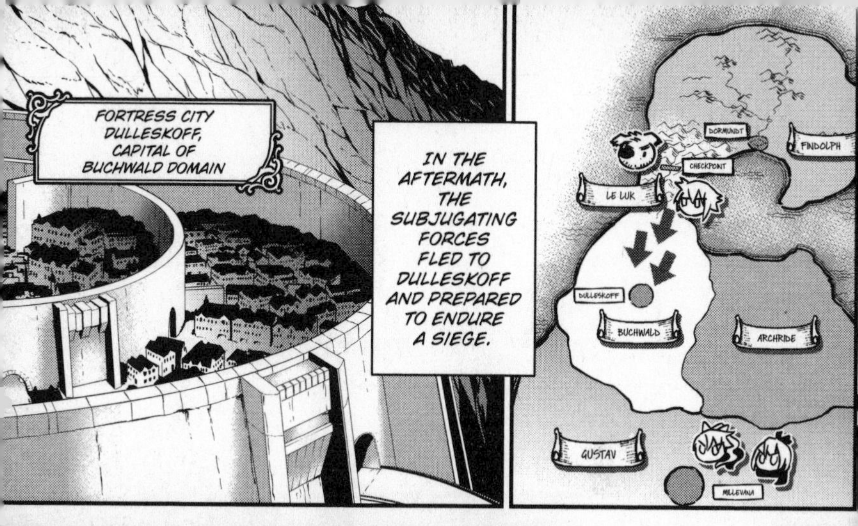

BY WAY OF THIS ATTACK, THE SEVEN LUMINARIES CONVEYED TO ARCHRIDE AND HIS PEOPLE...

...THAT EVEN MIGHTY FORTRESS WALLS WOULD PROVE NO OBSTACLE FOR THEM.

THE SEVEN LUMINARIES ADVISED DISARMAMENT AND UNCONDITIONAL SURRENDER.
WITH THAT, BOTH BUCHWALD AND ARCHRIDE DOMAINS CAME UNDER THEIR CONTROL—
ALL WITHIN A MERE WEEK FROM THE OPENING OF HOSTILITIES IN THE LE LUK MOUNTAINS.

HIGH SCHOOL
PRODIGIES HAVE
IT EASY EVEN IN
ANOTHER
WORLD!

CHARACTER FILE 14

Marquis Archride & Marquis Buchwald

Under Gustav's orders, these two led a joint coalition in the hopes of quashing the Seven Luminaries. Archride is known as the "shrewd general of the north," while Buchwald is no more than his flunky.

HARD TO BELIEVE, HUH?
FINDOLPH AND THAT STOOGE BUCHWALD ARE ONE THING, BUT...
...EVEN ARCHRIDE'S ARMORED CAVALRY GOT WIPED OUT IN SECONDS?
STILL, FOR US AT THE BOTTOM, IT ALL WORKS IN OUR FAVOR.

I HEAR THEY ALREADY ROUNDED UP THE CORRUPT NOBLES.
HA-HA! LOVE TO HEAR THAT!
IT STILL SEEMS UNREAL.
NOBLES ACTUALLY UNDER ARREST FOR HARMING COMMON-ERS...?

IT'S ALL THANKS TO THE GREAT AND WISE SEVEN LUMINARIES.
YOU KNOW THE EMPEROR WON'T JUST SIT ON HIS HANDS AND GO DOWN WITHOUT A FIGHT, BUT...
...I HOPE THESE GUYS CAN WIN... AND REALLY USHER IN A NEW ERA.

CHAPTER 31: DIVINE MIRACLE

INDUSTRIAL DISTRICT, DORMUNDT OUTSKIRTS
ONE WEEK AFTER THE BATTLE BETWEEN THE SEVEN LUMINARIES AND THE SUBJUGATING ARMY...
...MARQUISES BUCHWALD AND ARCHRIDE, BOTH SEIZED BY THE SEVEN LUMINARIES...
...WERE INVITED TO TOUR DORMUNDT'S FACTORIES.
TH-THIS CAN'T BE!
RIFLING ...!
LIKE THE IMPERIAL WORK-SHOP'S LATEST!
WELCOME. THANK YOU BOTH FOR COMING...
...MARQUIS ARCHRIDE...
...MARQUIS BUCHWALD.
HEI-SER-AAT, SIR.
FORMER MAYOR OF DORMUNDT AND CURRENT MINISTER OF FINDOLPH PROVINCE WALTER VON HEISERAAT
RULER OF BUCHWALD DOMAIN MARQUIS BUCHWALD

AS AN ACTIVE MILITARY LEADER, IT STANDS TO REASON...
...THAT YOU WOULD HAVE ALREADY KNOWN OF RIFLING, MARQUIS ARCHRIDE.
R-RAI-FLING...? WHAT IS THAT?
RIFLING REFERS TO THE SPIRALING GROOVES WITHIN THE BARREL OF A FIREARM.
THIS PUTS SPIN ON THE BULLET, ALLOWING FOR STABILIZED SHOTS THAT FLY FARTHER.
THE EMPIRE HALTED DEVELOPMENT SINCE THE TECHNOLOGY IS TOUGH TO CREATE AND COSTLY.
NEVER GUESSED THEY WERE MASS-PRODUCING THESE GUNS HERE...
WE HOPE TO HAVE THE ENTIRE ORDER OF THE SEVEN LUMINARIES EQUIPPED WITH RIFLES.
AND IT'S ALL THANKS TO THESE FACILITIES, GRANTED TO US BY GOD AKATSUKI OF THE SEVEN LUMINARIES.
THE VARIOUS MACHINERY ALLOW US TO PRODUCE INTRICATE PARTS WITH EASE.

FOR THE EMPIRE'S ARTISANS TO CRAFT GUN BARRELS ...
...THEY MUST FORGE IRON PLATES, ROUND THEM, AND WRAP THEM IN A LAYER OF STEEL.
IT'S A GRUELING PROCESS THAT DEMANDS A LOT.
BUT HERE, A DRILL IS USED TO TURN THE STEEL TUBES INTO GUN BARRELS WITH RIFLING.

NATURALLY, THIS SAVES AN INCREDIBLE AMOUNT OF TIME IN GUN BARREL PRODUCTION.
SO THAT EXPLAINS THE SECRET BEHIND THE VAST NUMBER OF GUNS AND THEIR LONG RANGE...
BUT WHAT OF THE RAPID FIRE?
WAS THAT MORE DIVINE PROVIDENCE?

THE KEY TO THAT RAPID FIRE ARE THESE.
SU (SHP)
WHAT ARE THEY? THORNS? ARROW-HEADS?

THAT, MY FRIEND, IS A BULLET.
A BULLET!? THIS ENORMOUS METAL SPIKE!?
YES... WELL, JUST THE TIP OF IT.
JUST THE TIP? WHAT ABOUT THE REST?

THE REST OF THE SHELL IS HOLLOW AND FILLED WITH *A CERTAIN SOMETHING*.
MARQUIS ARCHRIDE, ANY GUESS AS TO WHAT THAT MIGHT BE?
COULD IT BE...GUNPOWDER?

PRECISELY... BY COMBINING THE TWO, WE SAVE THE TIME IT WOULD TAKE TO INSERT FRESH POWDER.
THEN, THE SYSTEM OF SPRINGS AND MECHANISMS...
ジャキーン
JAKIN (KACHAK)

JAKIN
DON (BLAM)
...ALLOWS FOR RAPID FIRE.
DON
JAKIN
DON
...WHAT A FANTASTIC CONCEPT ......!
DON
B-BUT... HANG ON!
SO JUST LIKE THE EMPIRE, YOU'RE USING GUNPOWDER TO PUMP OUT THE BULLETS, RIGHT!?
YES.
THAT DOESN'T MAKE SENSE!
YOUR TROOPS MUST'VE FIRED THOUSANDS OF ROUNDS!!
WHERE IN THE WORLD DID YOU OBTAIN SUCH A VAST AMOUNT OF GUN-POWDER!?

INDEED! FINDOLPH NEVER SEEMED ENTHUSIASTIC ABOUT ARMING HIS TROOPS WITH FIREARMS.
AND THE RAW MATERIAL FOR GUNPOWDER, SALTPETER, IS NOT A COMMON COMMODITY.
...CHALK THAT ONE UP TO A DIVINE MIRACLE.
MIRA-CLE?

THE ANGEL WHO BUILT THESE FACILITIES HAS A RETAINER, AND THE CREATURE EXPLAINED IT TO US...
...SAYING THAT BY DIVINE MIRACLES...
...OR IN ESSENCE, BY MAGIC, THEY CREATED GUNPOWDER FROM THIN AIR.
TH-THIN AIR!?
THEY REALLY WHIPPED UP GUN-POWDER FROM NOTHING AT ALL!?
IS THAT EVEN POSSIBLE...?
IT SEEMS THEY CAN...
...USING A DIVINE SPELL CALLED THE "HABER-BOSCH PROCESS."
HABER-WHAT...?
Also known as magic that "turns water and coal and air into bread."

Put simply, heat and pressure cause a chemical reaction that catalyzes iron oxide.
This technique extracts nitrogen from the air, fixes it in place, and yields ammonia.
???
Ammonia, in turn, is required to synthesize saltpeter—the raw ingredient behind gun-powder.
??????

J-just think of it as a divine spell that extracts gunpowder from thin air!!
HAVING COME FACE-TO-FACE WITH OUR FRONT LINES, YOU OF ALL PEOPLE SHOULD REALIZE...
...THAT THE INCREDIBLE AMOUNT OF GUNPOWDER EMPLOYED BY THE ORDER OF THE SEVEN LUMINARIES...
...COULD ONLY BE THE RESULT OF A DIVINE MIRACLE.
THIS IS A LOT TO TAKE IN...!

THESE SEVEN LUMINARIES AREN'T JUST REBELLIOUS CHILDREN WITH ADVANCED WEAPONRY.
THEIR TRUE POWER IS GREATER THAN ANY GUN—
THE INTELLECT THEY COLLECTIVELY POSSESS.
BUT WHO ARE THESE BOYS AND GIRLS CALLING THEMSELVES GODS AND ANGELS!?

HAVE A LOOK, MARQUIS ARCH-RIDE.
WH-WHAT IS THIS?
IT IS A DETAILED PLAN DISTRIBUTED TO THE ORDER OF THE SEVEN LUMINARIES BEFORE THE BATTLE WITH YOUR SUBJUGATING ARMY.
TSUKASA-DONO, THE ANGEL SERVING AS OUR NEW GOD'S TACTICIAN...
...THOUGHT THIS MIGHT HELP CONVINCE YOU, MARQUIS.

ZO (SHUDDER)

THIS DETAILS NOT ONLY THE ACTIONS I TOOK...
...BUT ALSO EVERY OTHER OPTION I MIGHT HAVE CONSIDERED AT THE TIME.

IT'S ALL WRITTEN HERE, PLAIN AS DAY.
THE BOY MAY AS WELL BE A PROPHET.

HA-HA... INCREDI-BLE.
HA-HA-HA-HA-HA-HA......!
MARQUIS ARCHRIDE?

VERY WELL... IT HAS BECOME CLEAR TO ME.
WE ARE VASTLY OUTMATCHED... IN BOTH OUR THINKING... AND OUR FORESIGHT...
WE NEVER STOOD A CHANCE, BUCHWALD.

SOME-HOW OR OTHER...
...WE ACTUALLY WENT TO WAR AGAINST GODS.

AND WE CANNOT DEFEAT GODS. ARCHRIDE DOMAIN HEREBY PLEDGES ITS ALLEGIANCE TO THE SEVEN LUMINARIES.

SA (FWIP)
B-BUCHWALD DOMAIN VOWS ITS ALLEGIANCE AS WELL!

—SO WHERE ARE THESE GODS ANYWAY?

MILLEVANA, CAPITAL CITY OF GUSTAV DOMAIN
HEY, YOU FIND HIM YET?
NOPE. THERE'S NO SIGN OF HIM.

FIFTEEN HUNDRED SOLDIERS GOT WIPED OUT INSTANTLY WHEN THE CASTLE CAME DOWN.
HARD TO IMAGINE THE MAN AT THE CENTER OF THIS MESS SOMEHOW MAKING IT OUT IN ONE PIECE.
TRUE ENOUGH.
HEY, WE'RE PULLIN' OUT.

GUSTAV IS DEAD!
THE BLUE BRIGADE HAS BEEN VICTORI-OUS!

HIGH SCHOOL PRODIGIES HAVE IT EASY EVEN IN ANOTHER WORLD!, VOLUME 4 • END

TRANSLATION NOTES

COMMON HONORIFICS

no honorific: Indicates familiarity or closeness; if used without permission or reason, addressing someone in this manner would constitute an insult.

-san: The Japanese equivalent of Mr./Mrs./Miss. If a situation calls for politeness, this is the fail-safe honorific.

-sama: Conveys great respect; may also indicate that the social status of the speaker is lower than that of the addressee.

-kun: Used most often when referring to boys, this indicates affection or familiarity. Occasionally used by older men among their peers, but it may also be used by anyone referring to a person of lower standing.

-chan: An affectionate honorific indicating familiarity used mostly in reference to girls; also used in reference to cute persons or animals. Variants include ***-chin***.

-senpai: A suffix used to address upperclassmen or more experienced coworkers.

-sensei: A respectful term for teachers, artists, or high-level professionals.

-dono: A respectful term typically equated with "lord" or "master," this honorific has an archaic spin to it when used in colloquial parlance.

Page 13
Ringo's A.I. companion's name, **Kumausa**, is a combination of "bear" (*kuma*) and "rabbit" (*usagi*). However, Kumausa definitely favors its bear side when it comes to peppering its dialogue with puns.

Page 52
Aoi Ichijou uses the old-fashioned ***gozaru*** sentence ending in Japanese, making her sound like a samurai from ages past.

Page 160
Fritz Haber, co-creator of the **Haber-Bosch process**, claimed his method could turn air into bread. In truth, the process synthesizes ammonia from air and water, which is in turn used to create gunpowder and fertilizer. Fertilizer creates arable land, leading to better farming and more bread to feed hungry mouths.

CHARACTER FILE 15

Count Heiseraat

Former mayor of the metropolis of Dormundt in Findolph domain. He's an obsessive collector of rare imports, like the wristwatch Masato gave him in return for a trading license.

YAWN
A beary good morning to you, Ringo-chan!
MORNIN'... GOTTA WASH UP...
While you're at it, why not go outside fur some breakfast for once?
OH, SURE...
FURA (WOBBLE)
FURA
MMM...
High School Prodigies Have It Easy Even in Another World!
Extra
OOF!
BAIN (SQUOOSH)
KYAH!
OH, IF IT ISN'T RINGO-SAN! SO SORRY, I WASN'T WATCHING WHERE I WAS GOING.
L-LYRULE... SAN.
YES, IT'S ME.
CAN I HELP YOU WITH ANYTHING?
LAUNDRY, PERHAPS...?
I'M... GOOD, THANKS...

NEVER HESITATE TO ASK, OKAY?
THANK... YOU...
......
......
THEY'RE AS BIG AS EVER TODAY...
HOW DO YOU GROW THEM THAT BIG...?
HMM?

ワイ
WAI (CHATTER)
ばいんっ
BAIN (BYOING)
ワイ
WAI

ぼぃん
BAIN
ばぃん
BAIN
ばぃんっ
BAIN

C-COME TO THINK OF IT, THE WOMEN OF THIS WORLD...
GAAAAN (SHOCK)
THEY ALL... HAVE HUGE BOOBS...!!

N-NEED...
YORO (SWAY)
...TO FIND OUR WAY HOME QUICK...
YORO
AN-GEL!
RINGO!!
BIKUN (JOLT)
EEK!

OH. ROO-SAN... WI-NONA-SAN...
YOU FINALLY LEFT THE FACK-TREE, RINGO!
IT'S GOOD TO GO OUTSIDE TO DO BUSINESS SOMETIMES, Y'KNOW!
......!!
ぺたーん
PETAAAAN (FLAT)
RINGO, HOW 'BOUT COMIN' TO EAT BREAK-FAST WITH US?
AH... UM, WELL...
ばいんっ
BAIN (BYOING)
BIKUN (TWITCH)
WON'T YA COME?
WE'LL SPLIT THE BILL!
KOKUN (NOD)
MAYBE... WE CAN BECOME FRIENDS...
Did something pawsitive happen, Ringo-chan?
End

Thank you for purchasing Volume 4! That Haber-Bosch process is... out of this world! Historically, it was responsible for synthesized fertilizer and, therefore, the population boom, but it also turned warfare truly modern and is indirectly responsible for so many deaths. How will things turn out in the world of this story, I wonder?
—Riku Misora
CONGRATS ON VOLUME 4 OF THE PRODIGIES MANGA!
THERE ARE SOME EXPLOSIVE TWISTS IN THIS ONE— DEFINITELY WORTH READING! WOW!
SACRANECO

High School Prodigies Have It Easy
Even in Another World!
Special
Thanks
—Original Story:
Riku Misora-sensei
—Character Design:
Sacraneco
—My Editor at YG
—The People at
GA Bunko
—My Assistants

NEXT VOLUME PREVIEW
The high school prodigies take over the four northern domains at an astonishing pace.
DOON (BOOM)
DOON
Y-YOU HAVE MY GRATITUDE, SHINOBU.
Volume 5 on sale October 2019!

High School Prodigies Have It Easy Even in Another World! 5

High School Prodigies Have It Easy Even in Another World! 4

STORY BY Riku Misora ART BY Kotaro Yamada
CHARACTER DESIGN BY Sacraneco

Translation: Caleb D. Cook
Lettering: Brandon Bovia

This book is a work of fiction. Names, characters, places, and incidents are the product of the author's imagination or are used fictitiously. Any resemblance to actual events, locales, or persons, living or dead, is coincidental.

CHOUJIN KOUKOUSEI TACHI WA ISEKAI DEMO YOYU DE IKINUKU YOUDESU! vol. 4
© Riku Misora / SB Creative Corp. Character Design: Sacraneco
© 2017 Kotaro Yamada / SQUARE ENIX CO., LTD.
First published in Japan in 2017 by SQUARE ENIX CO., LTD.
English translation rights arranged with SQUARE ENIX CO., LTD.
and Yen Press, LLC through Tuttle Mori Agency, Inc.

English translation © 2019 by SQUARE ENIX CO., LTD.

Yen Press, LLC supports the right to free expression and the value of copyright. The purpose of copyright is to encourage writers and artists to produce the creative works that enrich our culture.

The scanning, uploading, and distribution of this book without permission is a theft of the author's intellectual property. If you would like permission to use material from the book (other than for review purposes), please contact the publisher. Thank you for your support of the author's rights.

Yen Press
150 West 30th Street, 19th Floor
New York, NY 10001

Visit us at yenpress.com

facebook.com/yenpress
twitter.com/yenpress

yenpress.tumblr.com
instagram.com/yenpress

First Yen Press Edition: July 2019

Yen Press is an imprint of Yen Press, LLC.
The Yen Press name and logo are trademarks of Yen Press, LLC.

The publisher is not responsible for websites (or their content) that are not owned by the publisher.

Library of Congress Control Number: 2018948324

ISBNs: 978-1-9753-0143-9 (paperback)
978-1-9753-0144-6 (ebook)

10 9 8 7 6 5 4 3 2 1

WOR

Printed in the United States of America